THE BIONIC PLAGUE

THE BIONIC PLAGUE

& other humorous
history howlers

heard by
Paul Sharpe

Dis Claymer: the speling, grammer and punkchewation in this book are as the children rote them, so are freekwently incorrect!

Illustration of the Iron Duck by Geoff Tristram

Cartoons by Carnegie

Text © Paul Sharpe, 2012
The moral rights of the author have been asserted by him in accordance with the Copyright, Designs and Patents Act 1988

Published by Palatine Books,
an imprint of Carnegie Publishing Ltd
Carnegie House,
Chatsworth Road,
Lancaster, LA1 4SL
www.carnegiepublishing.com

ISBN 978-1-874181-85-9

Designed and typeset by Carnegie Book Production

Printed and bound by Page Bros Norwich

Introduction

One of my teachers when I was a child used to say, "Every time you open your mouth, you put your foot in it." Mea culpa, both man and boy! And as an adult, of course, I am not alone – I clearly remember a colleague of mine, the head of French, who once burst into the staff room, flopped down on a chair and announced, "I'm exhausted. I've been giving orals all day!"

But though teachers and parents are a rich source of these gaffs, there's no greater goldmine than the writings and sayings of children themselves.

"A piece of graffiti has appeared on the wall of the changing room," said the headmaster. "It says I'm a CNUT. Either whoever wrote it is dyslexic or they recognise my efforts at holding back the tides of ignorance."

It took me over thirty years to gather the following collection. It proves beyond doubt my total failure to teach History to generations of children.

Paul Sharpe, 2012

Greeks & Romans

The Ancient Greeks were very good mathemagicians.

The great leader of Athens during the Golden Age was called Protazoa.

An offering to the gods is a lesbian [libation].

A Roman villa had hot baths,
a mosaic floor and was
heated by a holocaust.

Hadrian's Wall was built to stop the pickets in Scotland.

Aristotle was an Ancient Greek tinker.

Jason &
the Argonauts
brought back the
Golden Fleas.

Saxons & Vikings

The greatest achievement of **Alfred the Great** was that he burned the cakes.

At Durham they have the bones of the Vulnerable Bede.

At Sutton Hoo they found a belt buckle weighing a tonne. They also found some silver bowels.

Alfred's brother died fighting the Dames at the Battle of Ashdown.

The bravest warriors who died in battle were taken by Valkyries up to feast with Odin in Havana.

Wogan was king of the Viking gods.

Blancmange was the first man to go to Greenland.

The toilet [at Jorvik] is just a basket with no bottom in it.

Sweyn Forkbeard attacked England. This is because Ethelred the Unready ordered the mascara of the Danes.

 # Medieval Kings

The barons made King John sign the Magna Carta. They were angry because the taxis had gone up.

William I died when he fell off his hore.

Today we have something like the Domesday Book where everybody is filed away.

Henry I got married a lot of times because he had 22 illegitimate children.

Edward III got his chance to claim the throne of France when the previous king died with no hair.

Edward III was King of England throughout the Hundred Years War.

Henry V was born a mammoth in 1387.

[He was born in Monmouth.]

The Crusades

Two pilgrims escaped from the Turks and asked the Pope for a crusade to free Jerusalem. Their names were Peter the Hermit and Walter Mitty [Walter the Penniless].

The Seljuks usually wore leather gherkins.

In the Crusades the nights fought the turds.

One of the men who went on the People's Crusade was Peter the Kermit.

The Medieval Church

Four knights all killed Becket at the same time

?

so that he could not identify which one did it.

People who had sinned went to pervitory to have their sins beaten out of them.

The vows of a monk were chastity, obedience and poultry.

During the Interdict all the churches closed down.
The only services allowed were baptism of babies
and the confessions of the dead.

Bertholt Schwartz was a German monk who did
experiments with gunpowder and
primitive canons.

Roger Bacon was born in 1914 and died in 1294, which
in those days was quite a long life.

The Frankenstein Friars first came to
England in 1224.

Marco Polo

Marco Polo had to travel over terrible ground
and through dessert.

Marco Polo was born in Venus.

He met the Kubilai Khan, the grandson of
the great Imran Khan.

Medieval Warfare

A cog was a war ship with a mast, square sail, crow's nest, castles and udders.

Knights did not keep to the rules [of chivalry] very much and they were often bent.

Knights would never ride on a mayor, only a stallion.

In a tournament if you capture a knight you can claim his whores, saddle, weapons and armour.

Chivalry involved a knight being gallant, brave, protective of ladies and pies [pious].

To fire a mangonel catapult you had to pull back on this wench and off it went.

The English could not knock down the walls [at the Siege of Calais] but they had to starve the people out. So a year later the people came out with starvation. Edward III's wife Queen Philippa begged mercy for six burgers.

The English had some advantages [at the Battle of Poitiers] despite their lack of numbers. There were marshes and buses in the way which stopped the French overwhelming the English.

A longbow arrow had iron points and peasants' feathers.

After the battle all you could hear was the sound of dead bodies.

Medieval Towns
& Villages

Outside the town there were cripples, leopards and beggars. Everyone was holding a pomander to their nose. I was told these were filled with **sweat** smelling herbs.

Lords and burgesses were summoned to Parliament by the Ritz [writs].

All the villagers would get together and choose one person to speak for them. This was called a village mute [moot].

It would take about a year for a peasant to earn his annual wages.

Sheep farming became intensive since as labour
was expensive the tenants chose sheep farming as
there were little workers to be employed ...
also prices dropped because there were
little people to eat the crops.

The English sent wool to Flanders which
they turned into cotton.

The wool was sold to flounders.

Beggars were whipped and sent away to
their home towns by the J.P. which
means justice of the prejudice.

Cruel sports included bull baiting
and cockle fighting.

The Black Death &
The Peasants' Revolt

The Black Death was the worst ever plaque.

There were two theories [about the Black Death].
One was that it was BIONIC PLAGUE.

It took the people who died in the Black Death
three hundred years to recover.

After the Black Death people called flatulence went round wiping themselves.

Of the 4 million people [in England] only about two and a half people survived the Black Death.

During the Peasants Revolt a row broke out between Walt Whitman and the Mayor of London.

Geoffrey Chaucer

Geoffrey Chaucer earned a good deal of money
but spent most of it on books, good living
and gravel [travel].

Chaucer was a D.J. [an M.P. and a J.P.].

Among the famous writers Chaucer met in his
travels were Petrarch and Pinoccio [Boccaccio].

Magellan was the first sailor to circumcise the world.

The Age of Discovery

The fall of Constantinople
was a big blow to
the trading trade.

A French manurescript came into
Caxton's hands.

Columbus sailed in three ships, the Santa
Maria, the Pinta and Nina. These were all
caramels [caravels].

Sir Francis Drake was born in 1543
and died in 1546.

His [Cortes, the Spanish conqueror
of Mexico] final difficulty was that
he had to cross rainforest,
dessert
and mountains
to reach the Aztecs.

Drake was an experienced sailsman.

The Reformation

Martin Luther lived during the Reformation
period and was a Lutheran.

The Protestants followed a man
called Lex Luther.

Jesuits, like other monks, took a vow of
poetry, chastity and obedience.

Martin Luther visited Rome in 1510 and
was shocked at the
disrespectful behaviour
of the priests.
He was especially taken aback
by the practice
of smelling indulgences.

The Reformation was when the
church split into Catholics and
Prostitutes.

Henry VIII

Wolsey asked Pope Clementine for a divorce.

Henry VIII had six wives. The first was his mother, Catherine of Aragon.

Henry VIII was said to have written the song Green Sleeze.

Pope Cement would not let Henry VIII have his divorce.

Henry VIII asked the Pope if he could
have a defrost.

When Henry wanted to divorce
Mrs Aragon he got Wolsey to do it.
But Wolsey couldn't get
the marriage annulled. So Henry
wanted him killed or executed.
While he was on his way down
to be killed in London
he died in a car journey.

Henry VIII closed down all the monstertrees.

Thomas More was executed because he would not accept Henry VIII as head of English.

The Mary Rose tipped over and sank into the solvent [the Solent].

The Mary Rose sank because it had too many canines on it [cannons].

After Edward VI died, Mary I became queer.

Anne Boleyn had six fingers on one hand and was bee-headed.

Elizabeth I

Elizabeth executed
her cousin
Mary Queen of Spots.

Elizabeth I's moth was Anne Boleyn.

Elizabeth I did not call herself head of the Church. She
called herself Governor instead. She was hopping to
please both Catholics and Protestants.

One of the greatest events of Elizabeth's time was
the execution of Mary Queen of Scouts.

The President of Spain built his invisible Armada.

Sir Francis Drake sailed to Cadiz and burned some Spanish ships. This is known as the Singing of the King of Spain's Beard.

Raleigh named America 'Vagina'
in honour of Queen Elizabeth I.

William Shakespeare

Shakespeare wrote Macbeth, Hamlet and
Gilbert and Sullivan.

Shakespeare wrote The Taming of the Screw.

Shakespeare wrote thirty-seven films altogether.

One of his comedies is
the Taming of the Shoe.

The Seventeenth Century

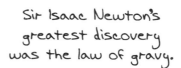

Sir Isaac Newton's greatest discovery was the law of gravy.

Charles I's official painter was Dick Van Dyke.

The picture shows Careles the First being executed.

Samuel Pepys began his famous dairy in 1660.

If it wasn't for Newton
discovering friction and
gravity we would all
be floating about in space.

Guy Fawkes was found under the houses
of parliament with
36 barrels of gunpowder.
He was executed, tortured, tried for
treason and not allowed
to live near London.

Wellington was

The Georgians

Horatio Nelson's mother died at the age of nine.

known by his nickname, the Iron Duck.

Nelson won the Battle of Trafalgar Square.

The Prince Regent later became Gorge IV.

Ships' biscuits were made out of wheat, peas and animal bone dust. They were nearly always stale and had maggots and weasels in them.

Modern History

In 1831 Isambard Kingdom Brunel built the 702 foot long Clifton Suspension Bride.

When Scott reached the South Pole he found that the Amazons had already been there.

A biplane is a plane with two wigs.

Another example of a secondary source is reproductive weapons (replica weapons).

English, Music & other Subjects

Clarissa was the biggest carp
in the aquarium at London Zoo.
She looked enormous swimming around
amongst all the other
crap in the tank.

I went to a party on Saturday and we
had to make the girls into mummies.
We raped them in toilet paper.

When we do the spring cleaning we normally tidy our rooms, then I do the polishing and mum does the hovering.

Mozart's operas include the Marriage of Figaro, Don Giovanni, Cose Fan Tutte and Mucous Membrane.

Elgar taught
himself
to play the violin,
cello and . . .
. . . baboon.

41

**Mathew, Mark, Luke and John were
early flowers of Jesus.**

The correct name for the Golden Temple at
Amritsar is the Handyman deer [Harmandir].

The Archbishop of Canterbury, Rowan Atkinson ...

If a car runs you over and breaks your leg the
driver has to give you constipation.

**Mozart wrote the Messiah and other
scared music.**

The normal temperature of a person
is about 96 Celsius.

Any higher and you would have a fever.

After our return from a medieval castle in Sussex, I set a homework in which the children were to write an essay, entitled "My Day at Bodiam Castle."

One child wrote, "My Day at Boney M Castle."

The Religious Studies homework had been set. Year 8 were asked to write an essay entitled, "What good can come of Pope Benedict XVI's visit to Britain?"

One of the essays had this suggestion: "When he is here, the Pope will be able to beautify Cardinal Newman."

"Never be afraid to question what you've been told," I told my History class. "How do we know? What evidence is there to support it? Does other evidence contradict it? Does it make sense? These are the sort of questions you should be asking."

The following year, I was asked to take a class in Scripture, as Religious Studies was then known. During a lesson on Noah's Ark, a boy remarked that he found it difficult to imagine how Noah could have caught all those animals and fitted them into a boat. Another wondered what Noah could have fed them on for forty days and nights.

I pointed out that there are different kinds of truth.

"When we study History, we are trying to find the truth about what happened," I explained. "But there is a different sort of truth in Scripture. Many of the earliest stories in the Old Testament are myths. They may not be factually true, but they contain a moral, much like those in Aesop's Fable about the tortoise and the hare. The moral of that story is that however talented you are, you can be overtaken by others if you don't try your hardest. In the story of Noah's Ark, we are being told that evil behaviour can cause disaster, and also how important it is that we protect wildlife. These messages can be more important than whether the story is factually correct."

Then as a group we looked for more of these morals in the story. Next morning I was called into the headmaster's study.

"I've had a complaint that you're teaching Atheism in your Scripture lessons," he said. "A father tells me his son has said, 'Mr Sharpe says the Bible is not true.'"

I explained to the headmaster how this had been misconstrued, and added, "What I'm teaching them isn't Atheism. I'm teaching them to think for themselves."

He scratched his head, and replied, "Think for themselves? Hmmm. That's an interesting idea."

Quotes from School

On Wednesday afternoons, children attended an activity of their choice, such as chess or needlework. The club I ran was called Extraordinary Creatures. We would find out about and discuss one animal per week. Among the extraordinary creatures we focused on were the Nile crocodile, white rhino and blue ringed octopus. We would spend a pleasant hour drawing pictures and sharing facts about our selected animal.

One day in the year following my retirement, I visited the school and was greeted by a little girl, who ran up to me and said, "Hello Mr Sharpe. My brother misses your club, EXTRAORDINARY TEACHERS!"

One ten-year-old boy to another:
'Look over there. That's a virgin.
You can always tell a virgin.'

I turned around to follow his stare,
and saw that he was pointing at
one of Richard Branson's aircraft.

LEN

I was greeted by a nine-year-old boy as I
arrived at school: 'Mr Sharpe, come quick and
look at our room. We've been putting French
letters up all over the walls!'

It was my first year as a newly qualified teacher. The school was in a prosperous, leafy village in Sussex.

The headmaster, taking me under his wing as a novice, offered me this advice: Always leave a door open if you're alone with a child. However innocent and proper you are, there are people who will believe the worst of you if accusations of impropriety are made. Never allow yourself to be put in a compromising situation.

A few days later, as she collected her son at the end of the school day, one of the mothers introduced herself to me:

"You must come and have lunch with us some time. This weekend perhaps? And of course, you can have a dip in the pool. Do you swim?"

"Yes, I love the water, though I'm not a brilliant swimmer," I replied.

"That's settled then," she said. Then, in a hushed drawl barely above a whisper, she continued, "Don't bother to bring your swimming trunks. You'll find us very broadminded, if you know what I mean."

I'm still thankful for that headmaster's advice.

Pupil on school trip to Hampton Court: 'Sir, what river is that?'
Teacher: 'That's the River Thames.'
Pupil: 'No it's not. The sign says it's the River Trips.'

On a school visit to London Zoo a boy asked the teacher what the animal was that they were looking at.

'Read the notice,' he replied. 'Every enclosure has a notice telling you the name of the animal, and a map with the place it comes from marked in red.'

A little while later, he overheard a conversation between that boy and another.

First boy: 'That's a dangerou.'

Second boy: 'No it's not. That's not a kangaroo. It doesn't look anything like a kangaroo.'

First boy: 'It's a dangerou. See the sign –'These animals are dangerous'."

A ten-year-old girl decided to try playing rugby with the boys. When the ball was passed to her and she saw a mass of vicious looking boys descending on her, she threw it away quickly, screaming, 'No, no – don't pass it to me!'

'Don't worry,' I reassured her. 'It's a rough game. You're brave to take part at all.' I then noticed nine year old Alex listening in to our conversation.

'She's quite right, you know,' he said. 'There's nothing in this world as precious as a woman's body.'

During a lesson on the Celts, I was asked how they shifted heavy objects like logs. I told the class that they used ox wagons.

'Oh sir! You never give a serious answer,' said Fred. 'They couldn't have had volkswagens.'

It was Parents' Evening. I'd been meeting parents since 5.30 p.m. for short interviews to discuss the progress of their children. It was now just gone 9.30, and the final pair was just finishing, having had a glowing report of their thirteen-year-old. Mrs T. sat back and said, 'Going away anywhere interesting on holiday this year Mr Sharpe?'

'We've got a place lined up near Lake Geneva,' I replied.

Mrs T. turned to her husband. 'Mr Sharpe and his wife are into wife swapping in a big way. They're always doing it. It's a fantastic idea. We really ought to get onto it.' Turning back to me, she went on, 'You must give us the contact details.'

There was a silent pause during which Mr T. sat in stunned, speechless horror. His wife turned to him and puzzled at the expression on his face. It suddenly dawned on her what she'd said. 'HOUSE swapping! HOUSE swapping!' she cried.

**A former member of the teaching staff:
'I've taught that boy everything I know, and
he knows absolutely nothing!'**

Excuses given by children:

1. Why haven't you done your homework?
   Reply: I couldn't do it. The tide was out.

2. Why are you late?
   Reply: Mummy was in bed with a client.

LEM

I was supervising a Science lesson with a class of 12-year-olds for a colleague. The experiment had already started. Children had been given various wind-up toys: woodpeckers, penguins, apes etc. and had to race them along a metre ruler.

They were asked to time them with a stopwatch, work out the speed and write up the results.

A boy said, 'Mr Sharpe, my bird won't go all the way. What would you advise?'

Boy reading a book: 'Sir, there's a word here I don't understand. What's a hooker?'

'How do you spell it?' I replied.

'H-O-O-K-A-H.'

On a visit to Westminster Abbey, the guide was showing the children the throne where monarchs are crowned.

'Our present queen, Elizabeth II, sat there,' he explained, 'while the Archbishop of Canterbury placed the crown on her head. It couldn't have been easy for Her Majesty,' he went on, 'because the crown is very heavy. Does anyone want to take a guess how much the crown weighs?'

A hand shot up and a boy ventured, 'One ton?'

The class was divided into two teams for a game of History Challenge. Each child had to challenge the other team by asking a question based on the term's work. A little girl, who had a gold Minoan earring in mind, asked:

'What is there a picture of in our book, that's six inches long and dangly?'

'King Offa,' I told the class, 'was the only ruler in Western Europe to be treated as an equal by Charlemagne, King of the Franks. Has anyone heard of Charlemagne?'

A hand went up, and a boy said, 'Has he got anything to do with Chinese takeaways? I've heard of chicken charlemagne.'

As homework on Queen Victoria, a class of eight-year-olds was asked to find out about Prince Albert. A little boy came in next morning with a computer printout, his internet search-engine results. It turned out that a Prince Albert is a variety of penis piercing, apparently popular with some sections of the community, in which a metal ring is put through the urethra to pin back the glans. The website claimed, rather unconvincingly, that it was called a Prince Albert because the Prince Consort had had this procedure done at the request of Queen Victoria, who found that it made her husband's member smell clean.

This was one rare occasion where the teacher was pleased that the pupil had not bothered to read what they had printed off!

The pupils had elected their form captain, a little boy who took his duties rather too seriously and did his best to maintain order and good behaviour. I once heard him announce to the class, "We'll have none of that bad language in here! There's only one person allowed to use bad language in this class and that's Mr Sharpe!"

'What unusual material did the Vikings cover the roofs of their houses with?' I asked. The answer I was looking for was turf.

'I don't like to say,' replied the small boy.

'Do you mean that you don't know?' I asked.

'I know, but I don't want to say,' came his reply.

'Why not?'

'It's rude,' he said meekly. 'Can I write it down?'

He wrote on a piece of scrap paper and showed it to me.

It read: sod.

I had arranged a school visit to the Royal Pavilion in Brighton. The guide sat the children down in a room and told them a brief history of the building and how it came to be built for the Prince Regent.

'A lot of people ask to see the secret passage,' he said. 'Well, I can tell you, there is no secret passage. We've searched the palace thoroughly, and if it was here, we'd have found it. Of course, when you think about it, there was no need for a secret passage. The prince's mistress, Mrs Fitzherbert, could come and go as she pleased. Their relationship was no secret. And the tunnel connecting the Pavilion to the Dome, where he had his royal stables, well, that wasn't a secret passage either, but just a way he could get to see his horses on a rainy day and stay dry. So, I'm afraid that I can't show you the secret passage, because, quite simply, there isn't one. Now, are there any questions?'

A boy put his hand up: 'When can we see the secret passage?'

At one time, my duties at school included ordering stationery. I nearly collapsed one morning during assembly when a female teacher came up and whispered in my ear, 'I'm desperate for a big Pritt!'

A boy came across the word gulf, and asked what it meant. I explained its geographical meaning and asked him if he had heard of the Gulf War. 'Oh!' he replied. 'I thought that was the Golf War.'

'Wergild was a Saxon system of law,' I explained to the class. 'If you killed a man, you had to pay wergild to his family. It was the amount of money a man's life was said to be worth. If you blinded him, you had to pay a sum of money that his eyes were said to be worth, and so on. There were similar amounts for an arm or leg. In some ways, it was a bit like the compensation that a driver would have to pay today, if he injured someone in an accident. Does anyone want to explain the meaning of compensation?'

A hand went up and a boy ventured, 'It's those little drops of water that run down the inside of your window.'

A boy came up to me on the playground and proudly announced that the Pope was staying in his house.

"Who did you say was staying in your house?" I asked.

"The Pope," he replied.

"Did I hear you correctly?" I asked. "Did you say the Pope was staying in your house?"

"That's right," he answered, quite calmly.

"Do you mean the Pope, the one who's the head of the church?"

"Yes, of course," he replied.

Obviously the boy must have misunderstood who the visitor was. At this point I decided to humour him, in the expectation that the true identity of the visitor would become clear with a few more questions.

"Does he wear long robes down to the ground?"

"Yes, and a big cross on a chain round his neck," the boy answered.

"I don't think the Pope is on an official visit to Britain at the moment. Are you quite sure it's him?"

"Well, he's staying with us," the boy insisted.

"Really? Where does he sleep?"

"In the spare bedroom," was his reply.

"At your house in Hove?"

"Yes. He's a friend of my dad."

The strange truth is that the boy wasn't mistaken, and I was wrong to doubt his word. The Pope was indeed staying at his house in Hove. But it wasn't John Paul II, the then head of the Roman Catholic Church in Rome. The guest in the spare room in Hove was Pope Shenouda III of the Coptic Orthodox Church of Alexandria.

We were standing in front of an Easter Island statue in the British Museum.

'This is a moai,' I explained. 'There are thousands of these strange, giant stone figures on Easter Island, the most remote place in the Pacific Ocean. One of the first Europeans to see them was Captain Cook in 1774. Does anyone know who Captain Cook was?'

A girl replied, 'Wasn't he in Peter Pan?'

It was the first performance of the school play. A little boy of six was cast in the role of a Saxon guard. He had only two lines to learn: 'Hubba the Dane is dead! We took him unawares.'

He made a fine impression as he stepped to the front of the stage, with spear in hand, and announced in a loud, clear voice: 'Hubba the Dane is dead! We took his underwear.'

'Right,' I told the class. 'Open your books at page 12. Before we start, I'm going to give you a quick summary of what we've read so far. Tom, do you know what a summary is?'

'Pardon sir?'

'Do you know what a summary is?'

'Yes sir, it's one of those men with swords.'

A ten-year-old boy asked me if I had seen the film 'Titanic'. I replied that I hadn't and asked if he would recommend it.

'It's very good,' he said, 'but there is one love scene in it that I don't think you should look at.'

We were sitting in the study of Jack, the headmaster, which doubled as a staff room, when one of the teachers came in and said to the head, 'I got your wife spayed.'

'You did WHAT?' Jack replied.

'I've got your wife spayed,' he repeated calmly.

'Have you gone mad? How could you have got my wife spayed?'

'I told you. I've got your wife's spade. I've left it by your car.'

At cricket, a boy was batting in a strange style, holding the bat in an unconventional way, missing some balls, but sometimes scoring four or even six runs. One of the fielders, a thirteen year old boy, said to him, 'Your batting is rather erotic!'

I wrote the title of the English homework on the board: 'Wildlife Conservation.'
One little boy wrote it down as 'Wildlife Conversation' and duly wrote his essay. It turned out to be a discussion between an elephant and a lion.

Q & A

Question: Who was prime minister of Great Britain from 1951 to 1955?

Answer: Was it Bob Hope?

Question: What is the correct name for an ancient Greek soldier?

Answer: A hobbit [correct answer: hoplite]

Question: Which general sent the runner, Pheidippides, to tell the citizens of Athens of their victory at the Battle of Marathon?

Answer: Millipedes [correct answer: Miltiades]

Question: What is this a picture of? [The class was shown a drawing of people dancing around a maypole.]

Answer: Is it pole dancing?

Question: Who conquered the Aztecs?
Answer: Was it General Custard?

Question: What is typhoid?
Answer: Is it a kind of tea?

Question: Does anyone know the meaning of the word bachelor?
Answer: We learned about one in Scripture – John the Bachelor.

Question: What was the most important cereal crop in Roman Britain?
Answer: Was it Coco Pops?

Question: Which book of the Bible describes the end of the world?
Answer: The Doomsday Book.